Journey Seven

A collection of images from Travel Photographer of the Year

Travel Photographer of the Year Ltd - The Photographers' Press

Publisher/Editor/Author - Chris Coe
Editor - Karen Coe
Designer - Gabrielle Davies

First published by Travel Photographer of the Year Ltd,
20 Yew Tree Courtyard, Earl Soham, Suffolk IP13 7SG, UK
www.tpoty.com

First edition published in July 2015
ISBN: 978-0-9549396-7-0

Reproduced, printed and bound by:
Geoff Neal Litho Ltd, 7 Pier Road, Feltham, Middlesex TW14 0TW

Front cover photograph: El Tatio geyser field, Chile. **Ignacio Palacios,** Spain/Australia.

Frontispiece photograph: Mandalay, Myanmar. **Manuel Librodo,** Philippines.

Page 3 photograph: The Pit Cenote, Riviera Maya, Mexico. **Terry Steeley,** UK.

Page 4 photograph: Ilulissat, Greenland. **Judith Conning,** Australia.

Page 5 photograph: John Day Fossil Beds, Painted Hills, Oregon, USA. **Anil Sud,** Canada.

Back cover photograph (top left): Cenote Taj Mahal, Riviera Maya, Mexico. **Terry Steeley,** UK.

Back cover photograph (middle left): 80° North of Svalbard in the Arctic.
Joshua Holko, Australia.

Back cover photograph (bottom left): La Guajira, Colombia. **Johnny Haglund,** Norway.

Back cover photograph (middle right): Storseisundet Bridge between Romsdal peninsula
and Averøya, Norway. **Piotr Trybalski,** Poland.

CONTENTS

The pace of change which our planet is experiencing seems to be ever increasing, at least if we believe the news which is spouted at us 24/7 and the accompanying photographs which support those stories. Fortunately they are not the whole picture. There's another planet Earth out there, a beautiful one with untainted wildernesses and remarkable people. Some of it is witnessed here in Journey Seven, the latest of the Travel Photographer of the Year series, which is waiting to take you to places which are awe-inspiringly beautiful, untouched and unspoiled, as well as those which are feeling the pressure of rapid change.

Travel photography is often thought of as pretty pictures. Yet the reality of such a diverse amalgam of genres is that the grit and the beauty sit alongside each other, often not geographically far apart. Through the eyes of a photographer, skilled in his or her art of working with light, even the grittiest can look beautiful. So much published photography is dour these days and reflects the torrent of news about disaster and gloom as though, somehow, only the worst in life, the mundane and the dull are of merit and worth recording. What's wrong with celebrating the beauty in the world and the joy of the human condition as well?

Would it be outrageous to suggest that photography should dare to inspire? Inspire us to travel, inspire us to care about our planet, inspire us to celebrate diversity and difference between cultures, inspire us to aspire to being better photographers, masters of our craft? The Travel Photographer of the Year awards are remarkable for the diversity of imagery which are showcased and this, along with the accessibility of these images to the viewing audience, makes them stand out amongst a growing plethora of photography awards. Travel is for everyone, as is photography and, whether we shoot on a high-end professional camera or a mobile phone, we are all travel photographers. We can all aspire to be better photographers and to take the type of images in Journey Seven. That is, perhaps, the magic in these pages.

As you thumb the 108 pages, we hope you take the time to read the photographers' own words about their images. These stories give an insight into their skills of capturing the light and the photographs reflect this. To dismiss the art and craft of the photographer as just clicking the shutter is to fail to understand what makes certain photographs leap out of the page and embed themselves in our memory. Light, time and composition make a photograph. Capturing these elements creatively and effectively requires skills which take time and patience to develop and master. To fail to grasp this is to fail to understand the essence of photography. It is this which makes it art and the fact that a majestic photograph can be reproduced many times does not diminish this. To assert that photography isn't art is an erroneous and spurious assertion, missing the point completely, as well as being contrary to the literal definition of the word.

However, the label is unimportant. It is you who will decide if a photograph merits it, not by calling it art but by your response to seeing it. Does it move you, engage you, make you want to look again and again? Does it transport you to another place? Does it make you want to go there, to meet the people, to experience nature's majesty? Does it lodge itself in your mind? If the answer to any of these questions is yes then the photographer has succeeded in his or her creative objective.

So let's start Journey Seven by turning the next page and finding out which photographs most engage you. Let this celebration of our amazing planet inspire you. Look for the light, admire the way the photographers have captured it and allow their compositions to etch themselves in your memory. We will all have our own and probably different personal favourites - that is also part of the magic of photography. Which are yours?

TRAVEL PHOTOGRAPHER OF THE YEAR 2014

Lalibela, Ethiopia and the Himba of Namibia have been photographed many times yet, despite our familiarity with these subjects, Philip Lee Harvey's elegant images of Lalibela and the beautiful and intimate Himba images have captured the subjects in a striking way.

The two sets of images are shot in very different styles. The Lalibela portfolio uses the portrait format to show the depth of the rock-hewn churches and this is complimented by the photographer's angle of view in this difficult lighting.

The portraits of the Himba woman are beautiful in their detail and limited colour palette, capturing the tribal shapes and patterns in strong compositions.

Sponsors of this award:

TPOTY, Plastic Sandwich

North West Namibia. **Philip Lee Harvey, UK.** *Canon EOS 1DX with 105mm lens; f4.5; 1/640s; ISO 160*

North West Namibia. **Philip Lee Harvey, UK.** *Canon EOS 1DX with 135mm lens; f4.5; 1/640s; ISO 160*

TRAVEL PHOTOGRAPHER OF THE YEAR 2014

Philip Lee Harvey UK
Winner

I visited a small village in the mountains above the Kunene River that separates Namibia from Angola. The Himba Tribe are considered the last semi-nomadic people of Namibia. The women of the Himba adorn their skin with an ointment made from butter and red Okha.

North West Namibia. **Philip Lee Harvey, UK.**
Canon EOS 1DX with 90mm lens; f5; 1/25s; ISO 160

North West Namibia. **Philip Lee Harvey, UK.** *Canon EOS 1DX with 105mm lens; f5; 1/80s; ISO 400*

This young lady's name is Karijto, I was immediately struck by her dignity and obvious beauty. Being very aware of her self-image, she was keen to review the photographs and thus it became a collaborative process. What struck me as refreshingly unusual, was that at no point was I asked for money by anyone in the village; all that was asked of me was to consider buying some of the handicrafts that they had made to offer visitors.

Lalibela, Ethiopia. **Philip Lee Harvey, UK.**
Canon EOS 1DX with 70mm lens; f5; 1/160s; ISO 320

TRAVEL PHOTOGRAPHER OF THE YEAR 2014

Philip Lee Harvey UK
Winner

Left. Photographed at Biete Gabriel-Rafael (House of the angels Gabriel and Raphael). The serenity of this young pilgrim's posture seems to me in direct contrast to the almost brutal architecture carved by hand centuries ago.

Below. A priest greets worshippers at St George's Church. Lalibela is one of Ethiopia's holiest cities, second only to Aksum, and is a centre of pilgrimage for much of the country. The Church of St George is the best known and last built of the 11 churches in Lalibela; this 12th Century monolithic structure is sometimes referred to as the 8th Wonder of the World.

Lalibela, Ethiopia. **Philip Lee Harvey, UK.**
Canon EOS 1DX with 84mm lens; f5; 1/160s; ISO 400

Lalibela, Ethiopia. **Philip Lee Harvey, UK.**
Canon EOS 1DX with 45mm lens; f6.3; 1/250s; ISO 400

Above. A high vantage point was important to depict an overview image of Sunday morning worshippers at the Church of St George. I find it difficult to comprehend the amount of effort involved in building these churches by hand. To visit the 11 churches of Lalibela is a humbling experience.

Above right. Lalibela has to be one of the great people-watching places of the world. Foreign visitors are outnumbered by Christian pilgrims who travel from all over the world to visit this holy site. This image was photographed at the Biete Medhane Alem (House of the Saviour of the World) Church. I was drawn in the first instance to the dramatic shaft of light, and then waited for the narrative to be complete.

Lalibela, Ethiopia. **Philip Lee Harvey, UK.**
Canon EOS 1DX with 28mm lens; f5; 1/320s; ISO 400

YOUNG TRAVEL PHOTOGRAPHER
OF THE YEAR 2014

The creativity of young photographers is inspiring and often mature beyond their years. Samuel Fisch has chosen unconventional, somewhat mundane, subjects for his images but has demonstrated a keen eye for detail and a wonderful eye for, and understanding of, colour in his portfolio of the Venetian island of Burano in Italy, famous for its bold coloured buildings. He has elegantly captured the essence of the place whilst staying away from the obvious canals and boats to create a clean, cohesive portfolio.

Sponsors of this award:

Photo Iconic, Plastic Sandwich, TPOTY

Burano, Italy. **Samuel Fisch, USA (age 17)**. *Nikon D800 with 24-70mm lens; f6.3; 1/250s; ISO 250*

YOUNG TRAVEL PHOTOGRAPHER OF THE YEAR 2014

Samuel Fisch USA
Winner

Walking past streets in Burano that served as backyards for many of the islands' residents, I stumbled upon everyday objects - clothes left out to dry, gardening tools propped up against a wall, a lone trash can placed outside the entryway to a house. All were ordinary at first glance, but many of these objects were coloured just as brilliantly as the houses that served as their backdrops. I decided to photograph these vignettes of objects placed against the graphic colours and textures of various walls, as they capture the essence of Burano without depicting the boats and canals frequently seen in images of the island.

Burano, Italy. **Samuel Fisch, USA (age 17).** *Nikon D800 with 24-70mm lens; f8; 1/200s; ISO 250*

Burano, Italy. **Samuel Fisch, USA (age 17).**
Nikon D800 with 24-70mm lens; f7.1; 1/320s; ISO 200

Burano, Italy. **Samuel Fisch, USA (age 17).** *Nikon D800 with 24-70mm lens; f8; 1/320s; ISO 250*

Mykonos, Greece. **Georgia Mulholland, Australia (age 18).** *Canon 700D with 18-55mm lens; f5.6; 1/85s; ISO 100*

In amongst the winding streets of Mykonos, and all the luxurious white houses with polished blue doors, this run-down old home stole my heart. Imagine the stories of strength, young love and self-discovery that these beautiful cracked doors would have seen in front of them.

YOUNG TRAVEL PHOTOGRAPHER OF THE YEAR 2014

Georgia Mulholland Australia
Winner - 15-18 age group

Right. Freshly-caught octopus hung out to dry in traditional Greek fashion along a path between the sea and the seafood restaurants.

Below. After spending many hours scurrying through the lanes, archways and small staircases of Oia to capture its beauty with my camera, I climbed onto a private rooftop where I could take a deep breath in and fully appreciate the amazing view in front of me. I can definitely see myself lying in that hammock, relaxing the days away.

Below right. Santorini, being the last stop on my trip around Europe, gave me the peace to reflect on my life-changing solo experience, which presented many high and low points.

Paros, Greece. **Georgia Mulholland, Australia (age 18).** *Canon 700D with 18-55mm lens; f3.5; 1/320s; ISO 320*

Oia, Santorini, Greece. **Georgia Mulholland, Australia (age 18).**
Canon EOS 700D with 18-55mm lens; f4.5; 1/400s; ISO 100

Thira, Santorini, Greece. **Georgia Mulholland, Australia (age 18).**
Canon 700D with 18-55mm lens; f7.1; 1/55s; ISO 100

Inle Lake, Shan State, Myanmar. **George Warr, UK (age 16).** *Canon 7D with 18-135mm lens; f5; 1/80s; ISO 2000*

Shwe Yaunghwe Kyaung Monastery, Nyaungshwe, Shan State, Myanmar. **George Warr, UK (age 16).**
Canon 7D with18-135mm lens; f8; 1/400s; ISO 6400

YOUNG TRAVEL PHOTOGRAPHER OF THE YEAR 2014

George Warr UK
Runner Up - 15-18 age group

Left. This twilight image shows an Intha fisherman framed by his conical fishing net. He is employing the unique Intha rowing technique where one leg is wrapped around the paddle to drive the blade through the water to propel his boat.

Below. This shows young monks during a morning scripture lesson. The young monk at the focal point of the image caught my attention due to his keen enthusiasm for the scripture chanting. The monks originate from the surrounding Shan hills.

Left. Pa-O tribeswoman at her tea stall at the Phaung Daw Oo Market, one of the rotating markets around Inle Lake. She is smoking a cheroot made in the nearby Shan hills, and her coloured headdress and black tunic are traditional to the Pa-O tribe.

Below. This image was taken on an evening visit to a stilted village, which was bustling with people returning home. This Intha boatman and his family are washing after the day's labour, reflecting the importance of the lake to every facet of the villagers' existence.

Phaung Daw Oo Market, Inle Lake, Shan State, Myanmar. **George Warr, UK (age 16).**
Canon 7D with 18-135mm lens; f8; 1/160s; ISO 2500

Maing Thauk Village, Inle Lake, Shan State, Myanmar. **George Warr, UK (age 16).** *Canon 7D with 18-135mm lens; f5.6; 1/100s; ISO 100*

Yogyakarta, Java, Indonesia. **Michael Theodric, Indonesia (age 12).** *Canon 5D II with 17-40mm lens; f8; 1/160s; ISO 100*

YOUNG TRAVEL PHOTOGRAPHER OF THE YEAR 2014

Michael Theodric, Indonesia
Winner - under 14 age group

Malang, Indonesia. **Michael Theodric, Indonesia (age 12).** *Canon 5D II with 70-200mm lens; f16; 1/50s; ISO 100*

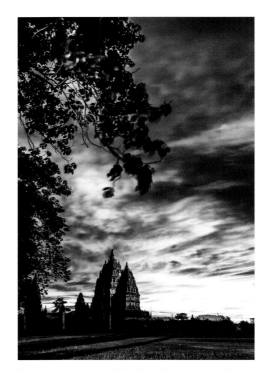

Yogyakarta, Java, Indonesia. **Michael Theodric, Indonesia (age 12).**
Canon 5D II with 17-40mm lens; f11; 30s; ISO 100

Opposite page top. Mount Merapi is an active volcano. It is very beautiful, but very dangerous when it erupts. Hundreds of people were killed in the 2010 eruption.

Opposite page below left. Borobudur Temple is a 9th century Buddhist temple, and also a UNESCO World Heritage site. It is the world's largest Buddhist temple. I took this picture from Punthuk Setumbu.

Opposite page below left. Prambanan Temple is one of the UNESCO World Heritage sites. It is a Hindu Temple.

Right. For me, this old woman has a hard life. She carried plants weighing almost 100 pounds to feed her animals. The background is Mount Merapi.

Yogyakarta, Java, Indonesia. **Michael Theodric, Indonesia (age 12).** *Canon 5D II with 17-40mm lens; f7.1; 1/500s; ISO 100*

Aswan, Egypt. **Arthur Allen, UK (age 10).**
Canon EOS 1100 with 18-51mm lens; f5.6; 1/60s; ISO 3200

YOUNG TRAVEL PHOTOGRAPHER OF THE YEAR 2014

Arthur Allen UK
Runner Up - under 14 age group

Left. This is a mummified crocodile in the Temple of Kom Ombo. The temple is dedicated to the crocodile god Sobek and there are images of crocodiles everywhere. I loved the way there were mummies of animals, not just humans. It is ancient and yet looking right at me.

Below. These are three beautiful baby crocodiles belonging to a man in Aswan. When I asked him what he would do with them, he told me he would put them back into the Nile, so that they would grow big and eat people.

Aswan, Egypt. **Arthur Allen, UK (age 10).** *Canon Powershot SX120 with 6-60mm lens; f2.8; 1/80s; ISO 80*

Aldeburgh beach, Suffolk, UK. **Will Jenkins, UK (age 11).** *Canon 5D II with 24-105mm lens; f5; 1/1250s; ISO 125*

YOUNG TRAVEL PHOTOGRAPHER
OF THE YEAR 2014

Will Jenkins UK
Runner Up - under 14 age group

Above. A golden retriever looking out to sea against a big sky, with a man texting on the beach in the background. A very modern beach scene. You don't know what the dog is waiting for or looking at.

Right. A very British-looking smart gentleman wearing a hat and having a drink, by his accessories of a guitar and plastic rubber rings. There are young men next to him in their swimming costumes and one is looking directly at the camera.

Aldeburgh beach, Suffolk, UK. **Will Jenkins, UK (age 11).**
Canon 5D II with 24-105mm lens; f7.1; 1/1250s; ISO 200

EARTH, AIR, FIRE, WATER
PORTFOLIO 2014

Formed and shaped by the elements, the many and varied landscapes change with time, climate, weather and natural events.

Simplicity is the defining element of Marsel van Oosten's winning images of dead camelthorn trees in the Namib Desert. Enhanced by the use of B&W, they use space and form to convey the harshness of the environment and the fading majesty of the trees in artistic images with the quality of fine pencil drawings.

Sponsor of this award:
Cutty Sark Blended Scotch Whisky

Deadvlei, Namib-Naukluft National Park, Namibia. **Marsel van Oosten, Netherlands.** *Nikon D4 with 24-70mm lens; f13; 8s; ISO 100*

Deadvlei, Namib-Naukluft National Park, Namibia. **Marsel van Oosten, Netherlands.** *Nikon D4 with 24-70mm lens; f11; 1/5s; ISO 100*

EARTH, AIR, FIRE, WATER
PORTFOLIO 2014

Marsel van Oosten Netherlands
Winner

Fog occurs only a few times each year in Deadvlei, which is
why I had to wait for many years to be able to photograph it.
The fog created wonderful low contrast light and it greatly
added to the surreal atmosphere.

Deadvlei, Namib-Naukluft National Park, Namibia. **Marsel van Oosten, Netherlands.** *Nikon D4 with 24-70mm lens; f11; 1/15s; ISO 100*

Deadvlei, Namib-Naukluft National Park, Namibia. **Marsel van Oosten, Netherlands.** *Nikon D4 with 24-70mm lens; f13; 1.3s; ISO 100*

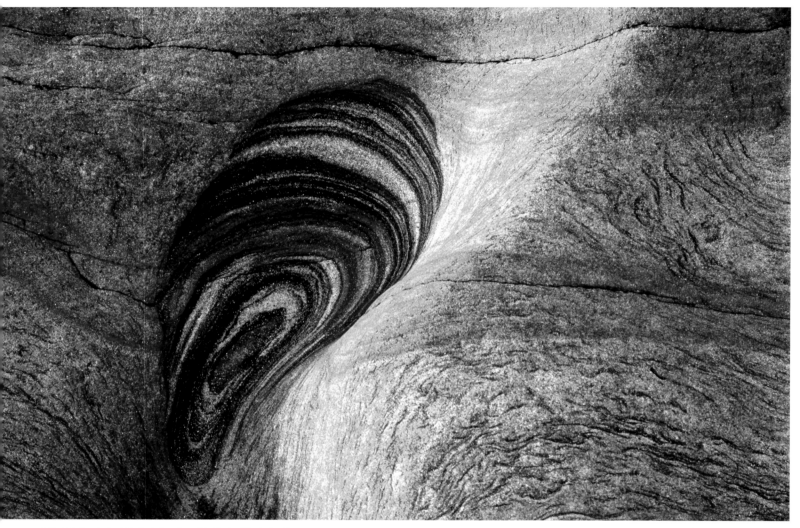

Spittal, Northumberland, England. **Peter Karry, UK.** *Minolta 9Xi with 24-105mm lens; f16; 1/15s; ISO 100*

EARTH, AIR, FIRE, WATER PORTFOLIO 2014

Peter Karry UK
Runner Up

In this picture, a shaft of sunlight cast a lovely bright area that reinforced the contours of the eroded stone below. Images such as this one epitomise the striking results that can be achieved in geology through the combined action of earth (chemicals acting on silicon), air (wind), fire (through fusion) and water (through erosion).

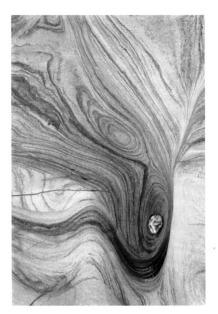

Spittal, Northumberland, England. **Peter Karry, UK.**
Minolta 9Xi with 24-105mm lens; f16; 1/15s; ISO 100

Spittal, Northumberland, England. **Peter Karry, UK.** *Minolta 9Xi with 24-105mm lens; f16; 1/15s; ISO 100*

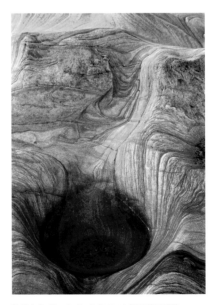

Spittal, Northumberland, England. **Peter Karry, UK.**
Minolta 9Xi with 24-105mm lens; f16; 1/15s; ISO 100

Above left. Looking at these wonderful natural patterns in this section of striated rock, it appeared to resemble a miniature valley hewn out of the surrounding hills of stone created by erosion. To me this showed an example of the beauty in the world around us, just waiting to be discovered.

Above right. These lovely curves caused by natural evolution combine with the symbiotically coloured rock which was placed within the image so that it helped to balance the result. Using bright colours in my photography has always been an attraction for me, so images such as this one draw my eye.

Left. Here a small rock pool has been left behind with some sand at its bottom. The details in these rocks can only be seen at low tide, when seawater is not covering them. Even then, frequently sand deposited by the sea partially covers them and you need an element of luck to find these rocks when they have been washed reasonably clean.

EARTH, AIR, FIRE, WATER
PORTFOLIO 2014

Ignacio Palacios Spain/Australia
Highly Commended

Below. Grey glacier is in the south end of the Southern Patagonia Ice Field or Campo de Hielo Sur, which is the world's second largest contiguous extrapolar ice field. The image was shot as a panoramic but in the end I cropped it square to make a stronger composition. It was shot at sunrise.

Torres del Paine National Park, Chile. **Ignacio Palacios, Spain/Australia.** *Pentax 645D with 25mm lens; f11; 0.6s; ISO 100*

Right. The sun was reflecting some beautiful light on the lake. This is one of my favourite photographs of the trip. It is a long exposure to blur the water.

Below. Salar de Uyuni is part of the Altiplano of Bolivia in South America. It took me some time to find a location with the right hexagon composition and without 4WD marks.

Perito Moreno, Patagonia, El Calafate, Argentina. **Ignacio Palacios, Spain/Australia.** *Pentax 645D with macro 120mm lens; f11; 27s; ISO 100*

Salar de Uyuni, Uyuni, Bolivia.
Ignacio Palacios, Spain/Australia.
Pentax 645D with 25mm lens; f11; 13s; ISO 100

El Tatio geyser field, Chile. **Ignacio Palacios, Spain/Australia.**
Pentax 645D with 55mm lens; f11; 1/8s; ISO 100

Left. El Tatio is a geyser field located within the Andes Mountains of northern Chile at 4,320 meters above mean sea level. It is among the highest-elevation geyser fields in the world. Its geysers erupt to an average height of about 75cm, with the highest eruption observed being around 6 metres.

Disco Bay, Greenland. **Nicolas Lotsos, Greece.** *Nikon D800E with 24-70mm lens; f9; 1/1250s; ISO 200*

Disco Bay, Greenland. **Nicolas Lotsos, Greece.** *Nikon D800E with 24-70mm lens; f8; 1/500s; ISO 200*

EARTH, AIR, FIRE, WATER PORTFOLIO 2014

Nicolas Lotsos Greece
Commended

Above. Project H.E.L.P. consists of two bodies of work: the coloured 'Hope Evokes' and the black & white 'Life Prevails'.

'Hope Evokes' is for the moments we sailed peacefully in the tranquil Arctic waters feeling confident that beauty of such magnitude cannot be vanished. 'Life Prevails' is black for seeing icebergs vanishing and white for their rebirth. The eternal play of death and birth, the dramatic circle of life. Life that finally Prevails, but only if we HELP.

Cape Kiwanda, Oregon, USA. **Thomas Haney, USA.** *Canon 5D II with 16-35mm lens; f16; 2s; ISO 50*

Hastings Fire, near Fairbanks, Alaska, USA. **Thomas Haney, USA.** *Olympus XZ-1 with 28-112mm lens; f5; 1/800s; ISO 100*

EARTH, AIR, FIRE, WATER
PORTFOLIO 2014

Thomas Haney USA
Commended

Above. The Oregon coast is hit by massive waves during the winter, many emanating from storms as far away as Antarctica. The biggest challenge in photographing this 200-foot long sea tunnel was avoiding them as they rushed through the tunnel and slammed against the rocks.

Left. Smoke from torching Black Spruce trees blocks out the sun on the Hastings Fire near Fairbanks, Alaska. My hotshot crew spent two weeks fighting this fire, which was dangerously close to town, and with the help of other crews and the weather, we were able to get it under control.

SPIRIT OF ADVENTURE PORTFOLIO 2014

The spirit of adventure is alive and takes us to some of the most remarkable places on the planet.

In Piotr Trybalski's images the cyclists are almost secondary to the striking light of the wild landscapes along the Norwegian coastal route, but serve to add scale and a dynamic quality to the images. Ugly tarmac roads are transformed into glistening strips of light, creating strong, smooth compositional forms through the rugged coastline and giving a sense of adventure into the unknown.

Sponsor of this award:

Warr's Harley-Davidson®

Storseisundet Bridge on Atlantic Road, connecting Romsdal peninsula with the island of Averøya, Norway. **Piotr Trybalski, Poland.** *Nikon D600 with 200mm lens; f5.6; 1/200s; ISO 800*

On the way to Dalsnibba mountain, Stranda Municipality, Møre og Romsdal, Norway. **Piotr Trybalski, Poland.** *Nikon D600 with 24mm lens; f6.3; 1/125s; ISO 200*

SPIRIT OF ADVENTURE PORTFOLIO 2014

Piotr Trybalski, Poland
Winner

Previous page. Windstorm, sometimes high waves breaking on the bridge and the rain - this is everyday life in September on one of the most beautiful routes in Scandinavia.

Above. At the end of the season, in September, Norway is almost empty. It's the perfect time for a challenge - to beat the road from Geirangejord to Dalsnibba mountain. It's almost 1500 meters in height and 21 km of sharp bends. It is a particular challenge, especially when the same day you have already covered more than 150 km of mountain roads.

Nibbevei road, Dalsnibba mountain, Stranda Municipality, Møre og Romsdal, Norway. **Piotr Trybalski, Poland.** *Nikon D600 with 200mm lens; f3.5; 1/2500s; ISO 50*

Trollstigen, Rauma Municipality, Møre og Romsdal, Norway. **Piotr Trybalski, Poland.**
Nikon D600 with19mm lens; f6.3; 1/640s; ISO 320

Above. Even in summer Dalsnibba is covered with snow. Until recently, the gravel road led here. Since the asphalt was laid, the place has become a cycling paradise. But only for the best. The reward is wonderful views.

Left. Cyclists climb one of the most scenic roads in Norway - Trollstigen. On the 10km long route, waiting for them is a climb of 10%, 11 sharp bends and more than 850 meters to the top.

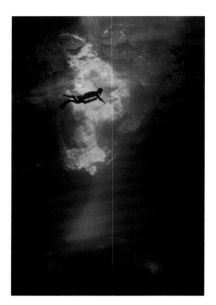

The Pit Cenote, Riviera Maya, Mexico. **Terry Steeley, UK.** *Canon 1DX, Canon 8-15mm fisheye lens; f9; 1/80s; ISO 3200*

Cenote Taj Mahal, Riviera Maya, Mexico. **Terry Steeley, UK.** *Canon 1DX with 8-15mm fisheye lens; f8; 1/60s; ISO 1800*

The Pit Cenote, Riviera Maya, Mexico. **Terry Steeley, UK.** *Canon 1DX with 8-15mm fisheye lens; f9; 1/100s; ISO 1600*

SPIRIT OF ADVENTURE
PORTFOLIO 2014

Terry Steeley UK
Runner Up

Above left. Explorers pass through a shallow halocline at 18 metres where the fresh and salt water meet. Descending further, they encounter an ethereal hydrogen sulphide cloud at 30 metres with tree branches eerily protruding out.

Above. Cenote Bill's Hole is only accessible by entering the underwater labyrinth at the Cenote Taj Mahal entrance and navigating the long crystal clear watery tunnels and a surreal, submerged 'lunar' landscape illuminated beautifully through the collapsed roof.

Left. In order to experience the kaleidoscopic show of spectacular dancing blue light shafts penetrating deep into the cavern, the sinkhole must be dived early in the morning before the sun has passed over the small entrance above.

Opposite page. The entrance of the 'Kukulkan Cenote' is truly a spectacular experience. Timed right, the entire cavern entrance lights up with a sensational curtain of animated sunbeams.

Kukulkan Cenote, Riviera Maya, Mexico. **Terry Steeley, UK.** *Canon 1DX with 8-15mm fisheye lens; f10; 1/160s; ISO 1000*

SPIRIT OF ADVENTURE
PORTFOLIO 2014

Marsel van Oosten Netherlands
Highly Commended

In search of undiscovered natural rock arches, I set up an expedition to the southeast of Algeria, close to the border with Libya. This was not without risk due to terrorist activity in this remote area. I added a human figure to give a sense of scale to the images.

Tassili N'Ajjer, Sahara, Algeria. **Marsel van Oosten, Netherlands.** *Nikon D3 with 14-24mm lens; f16; 1/250s; ISO 200*

Tassili N'Ajjer, Sahara, Algeria. **Marsel van Oosten, Netherlands.** *Nikon D3 with 14-24mm lens; f11; 1/160s; ISO 200*

Tassili N'Ajjer, Sahara, Algeria. **Marsel van Oosten, Netherlands.**
Nikon D3 with 14-24mm lens; f11; 1/320s; ISO 200

Tassili N'Ajjer, Sahara, Algeria. **Marsel van Oosten, Netherlands.**
Nikon D3 with 14-24mm lens; f13; 1/40s; ISO 200

Off the coast of Cascais, Lisbon, Portugal. **Gonçalo Barriga Portugal.** *Canon 1D IV with 100-400mm lens; f5.6; 1/3200s; ISO 500*

Off the coast of Cascais, Lisbon, Portugal. **Gonçalo Barriga, Portugal.**
Canon 1D IV with 100-400mm lens; f5.6; 1/2500s; ISO 500

SPIRIT OF ADVENTURE PORTFOLIO 2014

Gonçalo Barriga Portugal
Commended

Above. The Tall Ships Races is an international sailing competition, which saw its first edition in 1956. It brings together many of the world's huge training sailing ships in a celebration of international friendship while promoting the sail training of many young participants.

SPIRIT OF ADVENTURE PORTFOLIO 2014

Barbara Dall'Angelo Italy
Commended

I went back several times to the Masai Mara in order to try to witness the crossing of the Mara river by the wildebeest, and this year I was finally rewarded. That day a big group of wildebeest approached the river and after several attempts they finally decided to cross in a breathless crescendo. After seeing it, I understood why it is considered one of the most spectacular nature events ever.

Masai Mara, Kenya. **Barbara Dall'Angelo, Italy.** *Nikon D800 with 80-400mm lens; f10; 1/1000s; ISO 1000*

Masai Mara, Kenya. **Barbara Dall'Angelo, Italy.** *Nikon D800 with 80-400mm lens; f13; 1/1000s; ISO 1000*

TRIBES
PORTFOLIO 2014

As human beings and as fellow inhabitants of planet Earth, we have so much in common. As different tribes we have so many differences which make our world so intriguing and so worthwhile celebrating.

At first glance you can be forgiven for thinking that Nick Ng Yeow Kee's portraits were taken many decades ago but they are in fact charming contemporary images of a Han Community old people's home in LiuYi Village, Yunnan, China. They are intriguing and intimate, demonstrating the skill of engaging with the subject.

Sponsor of this award:

cazenove+loyd

LiuYi Village, Yunnan, China. **Nick Ng Yeow Kee, Malaysia.** *Sony A99 with 24-70mm lens; f2.8; 1/1000s; ISO 1600*

LiuYi Village, Yunnan, China. **Nick Ng Yeow Kee, Malaysia.** *Sony A99 with 24-70mm lens; f2.8; 1/400s; ISO 800*

TRIBES
PORTFOLIO 2014

Nick Ng Yeow Kee Malaysia
Winner

Previous page. This Han Community old people's home in LiuYi Village in rural Yunnan, China, brings us into a world of an ageing community, where the images are a reflection of the nation's history. Beneath the smiles, happiness and expressions lies a greying society that is being left out of modernisation; the Forgotten Faces of Contemporary China.

Above left. This series was based on a personal project, which was to shoot the 'Forgotten Faces of Contemporary China'. Along the way to the outback of Yunnan I looked forward to photographing the Lotus Feet ladies, and that was the planned destination. But this portfolio was born out of the journey, rather than the destination itself. It seems that most of the time, it is the journey that gives you the images you longed for.

Left. This particular portfolio was shot during a stop in LiuYi Village, where there was some sort of gathering among the old people. Most of the shots were taken as I sat down with them, enjoying their offer of lunch and Chinese rice wine. Each photograph has its own individual story. Every shot boils down to the friendship made with the people in them.

LiuYi Village, Yunnan, China. **Nick Ng Yeow Kee, Malaysia.**
Sony A99 with 24-70mm lens; f6.3; 1/160s; ISO 3200

LiuYi Village, Yunnan, China. **Nick Ng Yeow Kee, Malaysia.** *Sony A99 with 24-70mm lens; f7.1; 1/320s; ISO 800*

I was there for two days, before proceeding to other villages. I chose these four images based on the strong community feeling they portrayed, especially the group photo, which really stands out for me. The people in the photographs have all been together for ages, and I think the images show that.

Volakas village, Falakro mountain, Drama, Greece. **Nikos Vavdinoudis, Greece.** *Nikon D700 with 14-24mm lens; f6.3; 1/200s; ISO 200*

TRIBES
PORTFOLIO 2014

Nikos Vavdinoudis Greece
Runner Up

Above. Participants can be seen wearing masks made of animal skins, ringing bells strapped around their waists and having their face covered by ash. According to the natives' account, it's a symbolic call for a fertile and good year, full of fruitfulness and productivity.

Right. In this series I photographed the bell-wearers (Kodonoforoi) of Macedonia, a Dionysian tradition that has survived from ancient times in the Drama and Kavala Prefectures in Greece. This shot was made in an abandoned marble quarry. Marble mining is as old as the custom of 'kodonoforoi'; it dates from ancient times.

Nikisiana village, Kavala, Greece. **Nikos Vavdinoudis, Greece.**
Nikon D700 with 14-24mm lens; f7.1; 1/200s; ISO 200

Pirgoi village, Greece. **Nikos Vavdinoudis, Greece.**
Nikon D700 with 35mm lens; f4.5; 1/30s; ISO 200

Left. A family in an abandoned house at Pirgoi village. This photo shows the continuity of the 'kodonoforoi' custom as it passes from one generation to another.

Below. In some photographs, artificial lighting and settings have been used to highlight the person hiding behind the disguise. Here a white fabric was set as a background, a reference to shadow theatre that is also an old Greek custom.

Monastiraki village, Greece. **Nikos Vavdinoudis, Greece.** *Nikon D700 with 35mm lens; f8; 1/640s; ISO 500*

TRIBES
PORTFOLIO 2014

Arne Strømme Norway
Highly Commended

These pictures were taken on the small island of Hanimaadhoo, in the northern part of the Maldives. The population is mainly Sunni Muslims. This small beautiful island has more to offer than spectacular diving. Every evening before sunset the island's women and young girls come together on the beach to play different ball games. This particular group plays basketball.

Hanimaadhoo, Maldives. **Arne Strømme, Norway.** *Nikon D300 with 80-200mm lens; f4; 1/500s; ISO 400*

Hanimaadhoo, Maldives. **Arne Strømme, Norway.**
Nikon D300 with 80-200mm lens; f3.2; 1/800s; ISO 800

Hanimaadhoo, Maldives. **Arne Strømme, Norway.**
Nikon D300 with 80-200mm lens; f2.8; 1/400s; ISO 800

Hanimaadhoo, Maldives. **Arne Strømme, Norway.**
Nikon D300 with 80-200mm lens; f4; 1/400s; ISO 800

Burigoalini, Sundarbans National Park, Khulna Division, Bangladesh. **Tim Gerard Barker, Australia.** *Canon EOS 1DS II with 16-35mm lens; f4.5; 1/80s; 200*

Burigoalini, Sundarbans National Park, Khulna Division, Bangladesh. **Tim Gerard Barker, Australia.**
Canon EOS 1DS II with 70-200mm lens; f2.8; 1/160s; ISO 200

TRIBES
PORTFOLIO 2014

Tim Gerard Barker Australia
Commended

Above. A Mauali (honey-hunter) covers his face with a Gumsa to protect himself from bees during a honey hunt. This same area is also home to the Royal Bengal Tiger. The Maualis carry no protection against the tigers and are very vulnerable to attack.

Left. A colony of giant honeybees (Apis Dorsata) surrounds a comb of honey hanging from a tree. Giant honeybees are found in South and Southeast Asia and are renowned for their aggressive nature.

Burigoalini, Sundarbans National Park, Khulna Division, Bangladesh. **Tim Gerard Barker, Australia.**
Canon EOS 1DS II with 70-200mm lens; f2.8; 1/250s; ISO 200

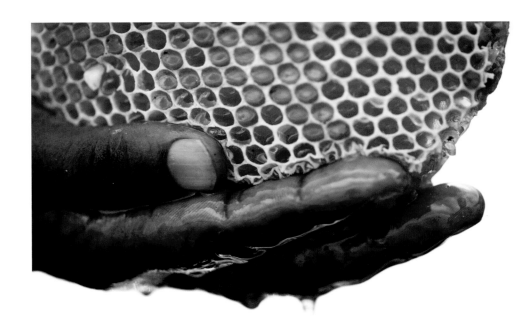

Burigoalini, Sundarbans National Park, Khulna Division, Bangladesh. **Tim Gerard Barker, Australia.**
Canon EOS 1DS II with 100mm lens; f2.8; 1/640s; ISO 100

Above. To subdue the bees the Maualis light a torch of dried leaves and branches to create smoke. This is placed under the colony to scatter the bees and allow the Maualis to cut the comb. The waxy base is left untouched and bees will return to rebuild the comb. Giant honeybees are migrational and they will return each year to the same tree.

Right. A honey-hunter holds freshly cut honeycomb. Honey hunting is possible in the Sundarbans each year between April and May when the bees migrate to the area. Honey is one of the most important natural resources to emerge out of the Sundarbans and each year over 250,000kg is produced.

ONE SHOT 2014
ONE MOMENT

Photography has the power to freeze a moment in time. Great photography captures a moment which lodges in our memory, often revealing something which the eye had not assimilated at the time or which was too fleeting to register.

Johnny Haglund's winning image combines the elegance of a portrait with the dynamic movement of the surrounding environment in Kinshasa, Congo. 'Les Sapeurs' have been brought into public awareness by the recent television adverts but this image returns them to their native environment, contrasting these sophisticated and quirky fashionistas with their grittier, more drab surroundings. The movement of the traffic elevates them as the main subject of this engaging portrait.

Sponsor of this award:

Railbookers

Kinshasa, Democratic Republic of Congo. **Johnny Haglund, Norway.** *Canon EOS 1Dx, with 24-70mm lens; f14; 0.8s; ISO 250*

ONE SHOT 2014
ONE MOMENT

Johnny Haglund Norway
Winner

Previous page. 'Les Sapeurs' are a unique group of people who wander the streets of Kinshasa wearing expensive designer clothes, despite the poverty around them. Although their appearance could indicate they are very different from other men in Congo, all the men in this image have kids and a normal job.

When I shot this photo, I wanted to capture the chaos around them. We were in downtown Kinshasa, with lots of noise, cars and people. But these men were still so calm and cool. I put my camera on a tripod and, with a long exposure, I got what I wanted.

ONE SHOT 2014
ONE MOMENT

Ly Hoang Long Vietnam
Runner Up

It was a windy morning while I climbed up Hoa Thang dune, where I saw local children playing with colourful kites on the top of the highest dune. They were all happy and amusing, and of course they quickly became my subject of shooting.

Binh Thuan Province, Vietnam. **Ly Hoang Long, Vietnam.** *Nikon D200 with 18-200mm lens; f11; 1/320s; ISO 400*

ONE SHOT 2014
ONE MOMENT

Germán Gutiérrez Spain
Highly Commended

Thang Hung was a child victim of Agent Orange. He was born with physical impairment; the disability affects mostly his arms. However, he tries to live a normal life: he got married, has two beautiful girls, has a breakfast restaurant and he´s the main source of income for his big family of nine members.

Hanoi, Vietnam. **Germán Gutiérrez, Spain.** *Nikon D7000 with17-50 lens; f2.8; 1/60s; ISO 800*

ONE SHOT 2014
ONE MOMENT

Ming Ong Singapore
Commended

What looks like a natural waterfall is actually a dam on a river in Bali. The locals bathe and wash their clothes here almost daily. The kids enjoyed themselves so much that it was like their private nature playground. Many have captured this scene umpteen times with a fast shutter, but I used a slower shutter to capture the arcs of water flowing from their buckets so as to convey motion, semi-freeze action, isolate subjects and smooth water while creating a dreamy effect.

Bali, Indonesia. **Ming Ong, Singapore.** *Nikon D4 with 70-200mm lens; f18; 1/20s; ISO 100*

Srinagar, Kashmir, India. **Marco Urso, Italy.** *Canon 1 EOS DX with 24-70mm lens; f2.8; 1/80s; ISO 1600*

ONE SHOT 2014
ONE MOMENT

Marco Urso Italy
Commended

The room was very dark and a dim light was hitting this fur merchant who was ordering his goods.

Sondrio, Lombardy, Italy. **Beniamino Pisati Italy.** *Canon 5D III with 24-105 lens; f4; 1/250s; ISO 400*

ONE SHOT 2014
ONE MOMENT

Beniamino Pisati Italy
Commended

A winter morning in the old town of Sondrio, in the heart of the Alps in Lombardy.

ONE SHOT 2014
ONE MOMENT

Bruna Brandão Brazil
Commended

Pedro is going through troubled times. He recently discovered a hernia injury that might take away his dream of achieving a dancer's career. This photograph was taken during a snowstorm, when he was out on a walk to clear his mind.

Essen, Germany. **Bruna Brandão, Brazil.** *Canon 6D with 50mm lens; f5.6; 1/500s; ISO 640*

ONE SHOT 2014
MONOCHROMAL

The absence of colour, replaced by tone, gives B&W images a unique power and impact.

Johnny Haglund's B&W portrait of an old Wayuu woman in La Guajira, Colombia, seemingly breaks the rules of composition but is all the more remarkable for it. In every line on her face and the wildness of her hair and expression lies the story of her life, more apparent and interesting for the absence of colour.

Sponsor of this award:

Railbookers

La Guajira, Colombia. **Johnny Haglund, Norway.** *Canon EOS 1Dx with 24-70mm lens; f20; 1/80s; ISO 10000*

ONE SHOT 2014
MONOCHROMAL

Johnny Haglund Norway
Winner

Previous page. An old Wayuu woman, not far from the northernmost part of mainland South America, on the Guajira Peninsula. She was inside a small restaurant, looking out towards the strong sunshine. Instead of doing the usual for a portrait, I wanted to try something different. So I used a small aperture because the background was just a white wall and it would not disturb the photo. I took several photos, but not until she raised her hand to scratch her head and at the same looked out towards the window, did I get my shot.

ONE SHOT 2014
MONOCHROMAL

Sue O'Connell UK
Runner Up

The Jember Fashion Carnaval takes place in an unlikely venue - a congested, commercial city in east Java. But this annual extravaganza galvanizes virtually the entire population, with participants vying to outdo each other in the most extravagant costume stakes. In this case, I was struck by the subject's complete poise and felt that his powerful presence and also the fantastic detail of his headgear would be best captured in monochrome.

Jember, Java, Indonesia. **Sue O'Connell, UK.** *Canon EOS 6D with 24-105mm lens; f8; 1/320s; ISO 640*

Mara river, North Serengeti, Tanzania. **Nicole Cambre, Belgium.** *Nikon D4 with 50-500mm lens; f6.3; 1/1600s; ISO 500*

ONE SHOT 2014
MONOCHROMAL

Nicole Cambre Belgium
Highly Commended

It was slightly raining so the wildebeest got confused and crossed the river in both directions. A small group of wildebeest was already at the other side of the river but crossed back to rejoin the large group that appeared to be moving on, as it was a too steep spot to cross. At the moment they were back on the other side, the big group changed its mind and started crossing. This wildebeest did not wait for its turn to cross but just jumped on top of the others.

Summit of Mont Gond (2,667m), Haute Nendaz, Valais, Switzerland. **Philip Field, UK.** *Nikon D7000 with 11-16mm lens; f4.5; 1/2000s; ISO 100*

ONE SHOT 2014
MONOCHROMAL

Philip Field UK
Commended

Above. Two mountain guides direct a helicopter into land high in the Swiss Alps during the Nendaz Freeride extreme ski and snowboard competition.

ONE SHOT 2014
MONOCHROMAL

Neil Buchan-Grant UK
Commended

Opposite page. I had gone to shoot the Feria celebrations on the outskirts of the village, but I found there were still many photo opportunities in the town, which was now quite desolate. I shot this scene without people initially, impressed simply by the strong geometry and contrasts. Then I waited around for a human element to enter the shot and give it some added interest. I only needed to wait about 10 minutes before the couple walked up the steps.

Vejer de la Frontera, Cadiz, Spain. **Neil Buchan-Grant, UK.** *Olympus OMD EM1 with 12-40mm lens; f2.8; 1/6400s; ISO 200*

ONE SHOT 2014
WILD AND VIBRANT

Everywhere we look the wild, crazy and untamed add vitality and vibrance, whether it be the struggle for survival or the exuberance of life itself.

In a time of environmental change the polar bear has become a powerful symbol of man's impact on our climate. The wildness of this image is evident but the image also conveys vibrancy, both in colour and in the sense of power and energy. The elegance of the setting contrasts with the gruesome natural way of life in this harsh environment of Svalbard while the two splashes of red connect death with survival.

Sponsor of this award:
Railbookers

80° North of Svalbard in the Arctic. **Joshua Holko, Australia.** *Canon EOS1DX with 200-400mm lens; f8; 1/1000s; ISO 400*

ONE SHOT 2014
WILD AND VIBRANT

Joshua Holko Australia
Winner

Previous Page. A large female polar bear looks up from a recent seal kill under the midnight sun on the edge of the permanent pack ice at 80º north of Svalbard.

ONE SHOT 2014
WILD AND VIBRANT

Marco Urso Italy
Runner Up

Below. These young bears were practicing fighting at the Kurile Lake, where dozens of bears congregate every year.

Kamchatka, Russia. **Marco Urso, Italy.** *Canon EOS 1DX with 500mm lens; f6.3; 1/2000s; ISO 800*

ONE SHOT 2014
WILD AND VIBRANT

Mike Reyfman USA
Highly Commended

Right. Parque das Aves is a conservation project that performs a valuable ecological service rescuing and rehabilitating trafficked birds. There is a small community of runaways living next to the park. These birds spent some time in huge aviaries and then somehow escaped to the forest. They didn't want to go far from the familiar place and were very accustomed to people. This Toco Toucan was so attracted by my apple and came so close that I could take photos with a micro lens.

Iguazu Falls, Brazil. **Mike Reyfman USA.** *Nikon D3X with 105mm lens; f9; 1/200s; ISO 400*

ONE SHOT 2014
WILD AND VIBRANT

Marco Urso Italy
Commended

Right. Watching the Red Crowned Cranes in Hokkaido I took this funny shot – shall we dance?

Hokkaido, Japan. **Marco Urso, Italy.** *Canon EOS 1DX with 500mm lens; f6.3; 1/1000s; ISO 800*

Himalayan foothills, Kaski Region, Nepal. **Andrew Newey, UK.** *Canon 5D II with 200mm lens; f2.8; 1/3200s; ISO 200*

ONE SHOT 2014
WILD AND VIBRANT

Andrew Newey UK
Commended

Using a bamboo pole known as a tanga to push the basket hanging beside him up against the cliff face, the cutter catches the honeycomb as it falls from the cliff.

ONE SHOT 2014
WILD AND VIBRANT

Jason Freeman Australia
Commended

Right. I came across this White-cheeked Turaco in a forest sanctuary in western Singapore. The colourful young bird landed just two metres away – seemingly as curious about me as I was about it. A dense tree canopy and fading light pushed exposure settings to ISO 3200 for this shot, handheld with a telephoto lens. Camera sensor quality, coupled with lens stabilisation, helped on this occasion – though it was the tenacity of the subject that made it possible!

Jurong Bird Park, Jurong, Singapore. **Jason Freeman, Australia.** *Nikon D600 with 70-200mm lens; f4; 1/90s; ISO 3200*

Angangueo, Mexico. **Tim Bird, UK.**
Canon 5D II with 400mm lens; f5.6; 1/250s; ISO 1600

ONE SHOT 2014
WILD AND VIBRANT

Tim Bird UK
Commended

Left. Every year, in the North American winter, millions of Monarch butterflies make the long flight south – over 2,000km – to these Mexican hills. When I made the climb up into the forest the sun was still rising and the butterflies were resting in vast clusters in the treetops. It took my eyes some time to adjust to the fact that these were not leaves but an enormous congregation of insects. When the sun began to rise, the wings of the butterflies began to open in the warmth and after an hour or two the sky was alive with a softly fluttering orange cloud.

NEW TALENT 2014
TRAVELOGUE

The art and craft of visual story telling is an essential part of photography and fundamental for up and coming photographers to master.

Cuba is a popular destination for photographers but so often the photographs which it yields are full of colour and marked by the clichéd symbols; American cars, music and dance, boxing and so on. This portfolio by Massimiliano Fabrizi caught the judges' eye because it captures the country's faded beauty and the more sombre side of its inhabitants.

Sponsors of this award:

Plastic Sandwich, Photo Iconic, TPOTY

Havana, Cuba. **Massimiliano Fabrizi, Italy.** *Canon 5D II with 24-70mm lens; f2.8; 1/50s; ISO 1600*

Havana, Cuba. **Massimiliano Fabrizi, Italy.** *Canon Powershot G11, with 28mm lens; f2.8; 1/5s; ISO 400*

NEW TALENT 2014
TRAVELOGUE

Massimiliano Fabrizi Italy
Winner

Previous page. It was a rainy day in Havana Centro when I walked into a busy alley full of cars and people strolling among street stalls. I found shelter under an old building's portico and watched the sky, waiting for the rain to stop. This woman was talking on the phone while walking up and down her balcony, gesturing with her arm and moving as if she was dancing.

Above. I was attracted by very loud music coming from a dark and empty street. I thought it was a house party with some couples dancing romantically. When I reached the door I found two lonely men quietly talking in a confidential way in a empty bar lit by dim neon lights, while the old radio was loudly playing 'Careless Whisper' by George Michael.

Trinidad, Cuba. **Massimiliano Fabrizi, Italy.**
Canon 5D II with 24-70mm lens; f2.8; 1/50s; ISO 125

Santiago, Cuba. **Massimiliano Fabrizi, Italy.**
Canon 5D II with 24-70mm lens; f4; 1/30s; ISO 250

Havana, Cuba. **Massimiliano Fabrizi, Italy.**
Canon 5D II with 24-70mm lens; f5.6; 1/125s; ISO 100

Top left. Trinidad is one of the most visited places in Cuba, crowded by tourists looking for colourful houses, fascinating courtyards and old churches. I avoided the downtown and started to walk uphill in the less visited outskirts, where buildings are run-down but street life is more vibrant and interesting.

Centre left. Many people were enjoying a fresh breeze sitting in front of their homes, the usual way to socialize with neighbours and passers-by. My unexpected presence in this street, while photographing a thoughtful guy walking back home, was quickly welcomed with some shots of rum under a pastel coloured sky.

Below left. Fishermen often gather at sunset on the seashore rocks facing the Malecon, selling the fish they have caught to street markets or to paladares, family-run restaurants often located in private homes.

Below. Malecon, the seaside boulevard of Havana, is a gathering place for people enjoying the last light of the day, while the sun sets behind the buildings. This girl was probably studying some university papers, while I was sitting a couple of meters from her. She hardly noticed me trying to find the right angle and take a series of portraits, helped by the sea breeze covering the shutter's noise.

Havana, Cuba. **Massimiliano Fabrizi, Italy.** *Canon 5D II with 70-200mm lens; f4; 1/80s; ISO 400*

Breidarmerkursandur, South Iceland. **Adam Balcy, Poland.**
Nikon D300 with 70-300mm lens; f13; 1/640s; ISO 800

The famous Jökulsárlón glacial lagoon area is one of the most visited places in Iceland. I have seen this place many times before however I always have the same fresh feeling like I am discovering a new place. The stormy weather is very common here during the winter and the ocean is extremely powerful.

Grundarfjordur, Snaefellsnes Peninsula, Iceland. **Adam Balcy, Poland.**
Nikon D300 with 18-70mm lens; f9; 1/320s; ISO 200

The lull before the storm on Mt. Kirkjufell in the last moments of sunshine before the snow descended.

Grundarfjordur, Snaefellsnes Peninsula, Iceland. **Adam Balcy, Poland.**
Nikon D300 with 70-300mm lens; f10; 1/1000s; ISO 200

Lake Myvatn, Northern Iceland. **Adam Balcy, Poland.**
Nikon D300 with 18-70mm lens; f10; 1/1250s; ISO 200

Lon, Southern Coast, Iceland. **Adam Balcy, Poland.**
Nikon D300 with 18-70mm lens; f8; 1/400s; ISO 400

Reyðarfjörður, South- East Iceland. **Adam Balcy, Poland.** *Nikon D300 with18-70mm lens; f8; 1/640s; ISO 400*

NEW TALENT 2014
TRAVELOGUE

Adam Balcy Poland
Runner Up

On this snowy and stormy day the graffiti hunter and polar bear on the wall were the only creatures that I met whilst passing the small town called Reyðarfjörður. Hunter and polar bear are not indigenous to Iceland; something we have in common I think.

Opposite page top right. The weather in my location was relatively calm while strong winds were whipping up ice and creating huge snowdrifts high up in the mountains surrounding Grundarfjordur fjord.

Opposite page centre right. This picture was taken while I was driving from Akureyri towards Lake Myvatn. Winter driving in Iceland can be challenging to say the least.

Opposite page bottom right. Typical horizontal snowfall due to very strong winds on the coast.

Lu Wenpeng, China
Highly Commended

Sao Felipe market in Salvador da Bahia is not only a daily market but also a community of the people who work and live there.

Salvador da Bahia, Brazil. **Lu Wenpeng, China.** *Canon 5D II with 35mm lens; f2.8; 1/15s; ISO 200*

Salvador da Bahia, Brazil. **Lu Wenpeng, China.** *Canon 5D II with 35mm lens; f2.8; 1/25s; ISO 200*

Salvador da Bahia, Brazil. **Lu Wenpeng, China.**
Canon 5D II with 35mm lens; f2.8; 1/25s; ISO 200

NEW TALENT 2014
TRAVELOGUE

Felicia Simion Romania
Commended

Right. A signalman relaxes between trains.

Far right. A railway signaller supervising the area.

Horsted Keynes, Haywards Heath, West Sussex, England.
Felicia Simion, Romania.
Canon 7D with 50mm lens; f3.5; 1/500s; ISO 320

Horsted Keynes, Haywards Heath, West Sussex, England. **Felicia Simion, Romania.**
Canon 7D with 50mm lens; f3.5; 1/100s; ISO 320

Right. When I was five years old, I dreamt that one day I would travel on a steam train. Now, 15 years later, I came all the way from Romania and had the chance to not only ride a steam locomotive, but also have an insight at the people who work and visit the Bluebell Railway in Sussex, England. I was fascinated by the genuineness and charm of the whole experience, by the workers' costumes and the kids' reactions to the ethereal experience.

Sheffield Park, Uckfield, East Sussex, England. **Felicia Simion, Romania.** *Canon 7D with 50mm lens; f7.1; 1/160s; ISO 160*

BEST SINGLE IMAGE
IN A PORTFOLIO 2014

Each year there are many portfolio entries which don't win prizes but amongst these are outstanding individual images. The best are selected from the portfolio by the judging panel and awarded the best single image in a portfolio or a judges' special mention. In 2014 these images were chosen from the three categories - Spirit of Adventure, Tribes and Earth, Air, Fire, Water.

Sponsor of this award:

Genesis Imaging

Baikal Lake, Ogoy Island, Russia. **Jakub Rybicki, Poland.** *Nikon D7000 with 18-200mm lens; f3.5; 1/250s; ISO 400*

EARTH, AIR, FIRE, WATER

Jakub Rybicki Poland
Winner

Previous Page. This picture was taken during a bicycle journey across Baikal Lake. Together with a friend I travelled over 800km on the clearest ice of the planet in temperatures reaching -35 Celsius. This photo was taken from an ice cave under Ogoy Island in the middle of our trip.

EARTH, AIR, FIRE, WATER

Marinka Masséus Netherlands
Special Mention

Below. A photo from the painting with light series, a series of long exposure photos. This photo pictures an abstract rendering of the harbour at sunset, where air, water, earth and fire meet.

Hong Kong, China. **Marinka Masséus, Netherlands.** *Canon 5D II with 70-300mm lens; f32; 1/8s; ISO 50*

EARTH, AIR, FIRE, WATER

Eric Lew USA
Special Mention

Spectacular lenticular clouds cast dramatic light on the striated snout of a glacier on the coast of Brabant Island in the Antarctic Peninsula. Diffracted light at the edge of the clouds creates an iridescent ring of colour known as irisation.

Brabant Island, Antarctic Peninsula. **Eric Lew, USA.** *Sony SLT A77V with16-50mm lens; f8; 1/640s; ISO 100*

Chambal River, India. **Patrick Griffiths, UK.** *Canon EOS 7D with 70-300mm lens; f8; 1/250s; ISO 100*

EARTH, AIR, FIRE, WATER

Patrick Griffiths UK
Special Mention

Several camels burdened with men sat atop stacks of wood plunged into the water from the eastern bank and waded towards the other side of the river. My boat chugged by at just the right moment. Opportunistic shots were taken quickly and somewhat awkwardly before the camels, their passengers, and their cargo disappeared in the haze of white behind me.

EARTH, AIR, FIRE, WATER

Nick Isden UK
Special Mention

Two men ride through a plague of locusts escaping the fields due to a bush fire.
Locusts threaten the livelihoods of millions of people dependent on agriculture in
Madagascar, but bush fires can be equally damaging to vegetation and livestock.

Antsirabe, Madagascar. **Nick Isden, UK.** *Canon 5D III with 24-70mm lens; f4; 1/320s; ISO 100*

EARTH, AIR, FIRE, WATER

Marsel van Oosten Netherlands
Special Mention

These whooper swans (cygnus cygnus) were resting on frozen Lake Kussharo. The sun was about to set, and as it was snowing, it got darker quickly. Suddenly the swans decided to fly back to their roosting spot.

Lake Kussharo, Hokkaido, Japan. **Marsel van Oosten, Netherlands.** *Nikon D4 with 70-200 lens; f8; 1/500s; ISO 800*

EARTH, AIR, FIRE, WATER

Barbara Dall'Angelo Italy
Special Mention

It was a starry night and Stromboli was erupting. I wanted to take in the same shot the violence of the fire together with the enchanted sky full of stars. The result is a sort of sky on fire in which the stars seem wrapped by the red smoke.

Stromboli, Italy. **Barbara Dall'Angelo, Italy.** *Nikon D800 with 14-24mm lens; f2.8; 22s; ISO 640*

Langtang, Nepal. **Timothy Allen, UK.** *Canon 5D III with 85mm lens; f7.1; 1/3200s; ISO 640*

SPIRIT OF ADVENTURE

Timothy Allen UK
Winner

Pilgrims walking up to Gosaikunda Lake at 14,370ft
in the Himalaya.

SPIRIT OF ADVENTURE

Arne Strømme Norway
Special Mention

The roads crisscrossing between the main traffic arteries in Africa are more mud than solid pavement. The minibus in which we were passengers had to stop every 500 meters to push and pull out of mud holes.

Bafousam, Cameroon. **Arne Strømme, Norway.** *Nikon D200 with 18-200mm lens; f11; 1/320s; ISO 400*

SPIRIT OF ADVENTURE

Anil Sud Canada
Special Mention

Full moon rising at sunset during the Austral summer in Antarctica.

Antarctica. **Anil Sud, Canada.** *Canon 5D III with 70-22mm lens; f7.1; 1/400s; ISO 1600*

Vatnajokull ice cave, Iceland. **Judith Conning, Australia.** *Canon 5D II with 16-35mm lens; f13; 10s; ISO 100*

SPIRIT OF ADVENTURE

Judith Conning, Australia
Special Mention

With some trepidation I entered the icy cavern, aware that there would be millions of tons of ice above. Within moments we were totally in awe of the incredible patterns and shape in the blue ice. Using tripods, low ISO and long shutter speeds helped create spectacular images. One of our party wore a very photogenic red jacket, so he stepped into the shaft of light with orders not to breathe until given permission. Flecks of red were reflected in the ice overhead.

Sinakara, Peru. **Timothy Allen, UK.** *Canon EOS 5D MkIII with 16-35mm lens; f3.5; 1/60s; ISO 1600*

BEST SINGLE IMAGE
TRIBES

Timothy Allen UK
Winner

Each year thousands of pilgrims travel to the Sinakara Valley, 15,000ft up in the Peruvian Andes, to celebrate the festival of Quyllur Rit'i. Here the pilgrims have an all-night vigil at the foot of the sacred glacier.

BEST SINGLE IMAGE
TRIBES

Tim Gerard Barker Australia
Special Mention

A woman sifts threshed rice straw to separate any remaining rice grains from straw. The entire production of rice is usually done by hand in Vietnam so as to maximize grain yield and minimize grain loss.

Yen Minh, Ha Giang, Vietnam. **Tim Gerard Barker, Australia.** *Canon 5D II with 35mm lens; f1.4; 1/500s; ISO 100*

Community Girls' School Shitindas, Gilgit-Baltistan, Pakistan.
Andrea Francolini, Italy. *Canon 1DX with 50mm lens; f1.8; 1/60s; ISO 800*

BEST SINGLE IMAGE
TRIBES

Andrea Francolini Italy
Special Mention

Close up portrait of Khizra. Five years old, she is the first student to receive a five-year sponsorship to attend class from grade 1 to 5 from My First School Trust. My First School is an Australian charity which helps promote and improve learning conditions in a remote northern area of Gilgit-Baltistan.

Mandalay, Myanmar. **Manuel Librodo, Philippines.** *Nikon D3S with 24-70mm lens; f6.3; 1/200s; ISO 8000*

BEST SINGLE IMAGE
TRIBES

Manuel Librodo Philippines
Special Mention

Monk walking in the hallways of Maha Aung Mye Bon Zan Monastery. Clad in a red robe, this novice monk was making his usual round. Anticipating the light coming from one of the doors, I waited for this moment as he approached that part of the temple. The wind added a drama as it lifted the robe thus creating a more pleasing form.

BEST SINGLE IMAGE
TRIBES

Sean Caffrey Canada
Special Mention

Pilgrims from across Ethiopia congregate in Lalibela during the lead up to the Orthodox Christmas celebrations. Lalibela is a holy city famous for the 13th century churches carved directly out of its volcanic bedrock. I noticed a priest reading a bible near this shaft of light and asked him to sit where the light was striking a bench.

Lalibela, Ethiopia. **Sean Caffrey, Canada.** *Nikon D800 with 1.4 art 50mm lens; f3.2; 1/200s; ISO 800.*

Regia village, Kibish. South Ethiopia. **Sergio Carbajo, Spain.** *Nikon D600 with 50mm lens; f1.8; 1/4000s; ISO 250*

BEST SINGLE IMAGE
TRIBES

Sergio Carbajo Spain
Special Mention

Portrait of a young Suri tribe boy in Regia village, Kibish. The Suri are one of the most remote tribes in South Ethiopia and South Sudan. The kids usually go to the rivers to play, painting their bodies and wearing floral ornaments.

Raven in Yellowstone National Park, Wyoming, USA. **Loulou Beavers, USA.** *Nikon D800 with 200-400mm lens; f5.6; 1.400s; ISO 500*

JUDGES

The TPOTY judging panel is international and made up of experts from the world of photography and travel. They are selected to reflect a variety of backgrounds, styles and attitudes to photography and the photographic image. A key element of the panel is the wealth of visual and specialist expertise brought into the mix by our technical and creative judges. Lay judges and past winners have also participated, bringing fresh views and perspectives to the judging process.

These judges give their time because they are passionate about photography, and we are immensely grateful for their efforts.

We would like to thank the 2014 judging panel:

Judges

Daria Bonera - *photo agency director and photo editor for National Geographic Traveller, Italy*

Barbara Bordnick - *photographer and lecturer*

Chris Coe - *photographer, author & lecturer*

Colin Finlay - *stock photography expert*

Jeremy Hoare - *photographer & TV cameraman*

Debbie Ireland - *picture editor & curator*

Eamonn McCabe - *award-winning photographer & picture editor*

Caroline Metcalfe - *former director of photography, Condé Nast Traveller*

Jerry Tavin - *stock photography expert and founder of Young Photographers' Alliance*

Emma Thomson - *award-winning travel writer*

Chris Weston - *wildlife photographer*

Manfred Zollner - *photographic critic and deputy editor in chief, Fotomagazin, Germany*

SPONSORS AND PARTNERS

Cutty Sark

Cutty Sark blended Scotch is an iconic whisky; its distinctive yellow label has graced the world's best bars and clubs for nearly 90 years. The first light-coloured blended whisky, it was launched at the height of cocktail culture in the 1920s and it has remained synonymous with enjoying great drinks in great company ever since. The brand keeps cropping up in popular culture, a constant reminder of the status of the brand. It is always the choice of adventurous characters! Cutty Sark's major markets are now Spain, Greece, Portugal, and the USA.

www.cutty-sark.com

railbookers
Holidays inspired by you

Railbookers

Railbookers are experts in crafting tailor made holidays to over 45 countries worldwide. Enjoy the journey, not just the destination and travel through the unspoilt vistas that embroider the world's railway tracks. Why not take the scenic journey of a lifetime through the snow-capped mountains and shimmering lakes of Switzerland? Snake down the spine of Italy from the 'Eternal City' of Rome to the Sicilian seas and sunshine or perhaps traverse the Rocky Mountains and prairie flats of Canada from the Pacific Ocean to the Atlantic?

www.railbookers.com

always extraordinary | **cazenove+loyd**

cazenove+loyd

cazenove+loyd are the experts in experiential travel. Started over 20 years ago by Henrietta Loyd, they create tailor-made trips to three exciting and challenging parts of the world, Africa + Indian Ocean, Asia + The Middle East and Central + South America. They also design a selection of intimate and exclusive small group experiences that offer unprecedented private access to some of the world's most inspiring places and cultures. Extraordinary experiences for every client.

www.cazloyd.com

StaaG®

StaaG® is a British lifestyle brand. The brand was founded by two Scottish brothers who grew up with design from a young age and British traditions in their DNA. StaaG® offers uniqueness and quality allowing you to demonstrate your appetite for exclusivity and an understanding of the traditionally modern British lifestyle. The StaaG products range from high end polo shirts to British hand made leather goods.

www.staag.co

Opposite page. Castellucio, Italy. **Barbara Dall'Angelo, Italy.** *Nikon D800 with 70-200mm lens; f13; 1/200s; ISO 400*

SPONSORS AND PARTNERS

Photo Iconic

Photo Iconic offers a range of TPOTY photography courses, workshops and masterclasses to suit all abilities and styles of photography, all tutored by award-winning photographers. These range from half-day workshops to one-week courses and include the festival of photography - Travel Photography Live - in association with Travel Photographer of the Year (TPOTY). Photo Iconic also runs the TPOTY Photo Tours; a selection of photographic holidays and adventures to some of the world's most interesting and inspiring destinations.

www.photoiconic.com.

Plastic Sandwich

Plastic Sandwich has been putting together portfolios for photographers and art directors since the early 1970s. It was founded by Joyce Pinto and Rob Jacobs - who has been with the company for over 30 years. Plastic Sandwich has had unparalleled experience in the field of image presentation in its various forms over the last 40 years and has been a proud sponsor of the TPOTY competition since 2003. Plastic Sandwich's services are also utilised by companies such as event and PR organisations, film companies, high-end presenters, and anyone whose activities or craft are best shown through the presentation of images. We are now direct suppliers to Jaguar Land Rover.

www.plasticsandwich.co.uk

Royal Geographical Society (with IBG)

The Royal Geographical Society (with The Institute of British Geographers) was formed in 1830 for 'the advancement of geographical science'. Today, they deliver this objective by developing, supporting and promoting geography through research, expeditions and fieldwork, education, and public engagement, while also providing geographical input to policy. They hold the world's largest private geographical collection and provide public access to it. In 2011 the Society embarked on a five-year partnership with Travel Photographer of the Year to host major annual exhibitions of the awards' stunning travel photography, supported by an ongoing programme of workshops and events.

www.rgs.org

Genesis Imaging

One of the UK's leading photographic image printers, Genesis Imaging is in the unique position of offering all manner of photographic printing, mounting and framing services for the creative industry. They believe photographic printing is an art. They print images of the highest calibre for some of the best-known professional photographers, artists and art galleries around – people who demand the very best quality available. Their superb Giclée Fine Art and Lambda prints have graced the walls of numerous famous galleries, from London's National Portrait Gallery to New York's Museum of Modern Art. Genesis Imaging print and mount all the Travel Photographer of the Year exhibitions.

www.genesisimaging.co.uk

Antarctica. **Anil Sud, Canada.** *Canon 5D MkIII with 200-400mm lens; f5.6; 1/500s; ISO 250*

SPONSORS AND PARTNERS

Harley-Davidson®

Warr's was founded on the Kings Road, London (England) in 1924 by Captain Frederick James Warr, becoming an official Harley-Davidson® dealer that same year. In 1949 F.J's son Fred Warr left the Royal Air Force and went to work for his father. Although post-War business was very tough, by the 1960's Fred Jnr had become Britain's Harley-Davidson® distributor. In 1999 the company moved into a new purpose-built 20,000 sq ft dealership built on the site of the original 1920s' store. In 2003 a further Harley dealership was opened in Mottingham, South London. From those early days up to today, Warr's has been synonymous with Harley-Davidson® and is Europe's oldest and certainly most successful Harley-Davidson® dealership Group. Today Warr's dealerships are still owned and operated by the Warr family and form a part of the Warr Group of companies.

www.warrs.com

Direct Photographic

With offices in London, Paris and Cape Town, Direct Photographic is dedicated to delivering the very best in rental equipment to photographers Worldwide. An active supporter of the industry as a whole, Direct Photographic is a keen investor in the latest equipment and remains committed to helping capture the vision of both emerging and established photographers. With an extensive range of products, including the latest in HD camera and LED lighting technology, plus continual investment throughout every aspect of its business, Direct Photographic is the perfect choice for every photographic project. Direct Photographic light the Travel Photographer of the Year exhibition at the Royal Geographical Society (with IBG) in London.

www.directphotographic.co.uk

FUJIFILM

Fujifilm

Fujifilm is a global leader in imaging technology, products and services including digital cameras, photofinishing, digital storage and recording media, consumer and professional film, motion picture film, professional video, printing systems, medical imaging, office technology, flat panel displays and graphic arts. The company employs more than 73,000 people worldwide, with 178 subsidiaries stretching across four continents. In the UK, Fujifilm has been supplying the imaging, printing and graphics industries, as well as consumers, professional and enthusiast photographers, with high quality, innovative products and services for over 25 years. All the TPOTY exhibition prints are produced on Fujifilm Crystal Archive paper and Direct to Media.

www.fujifilm.eu/uk

Esna, Egypt. **Arthur Allen, UK (age 10).** *Canon EOS 1100 with 18-51mm lens; f5.6; 1/100s; ISO 160*

INDEX OF PHOTOGRAPHERS

We would like to thank the photographers whose images appear in this book. Their support, along with that of all the other photographers from across the world who enter the awards, makes the Travel Photographer of the Year awards and this book possible.

Goroka, Eastern Highlands, Papua New Guinea, **Marinka Masséus, Netherlands.** *Canon 5D MkIII with 70-300mm lens; f5.6; 1/500s; ISO 50*

TAKE ANOTHER JOURNEY, JOIN US ON ANOTHER ADVENTURE.

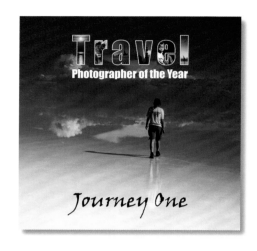

Journey One
2003-04

Journey Two
2005-06

Journey Three
2007-08

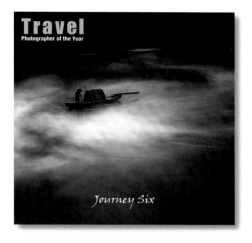

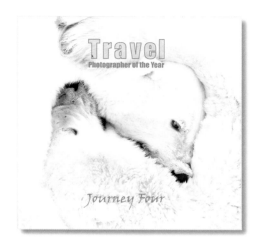

Journey Four
2010-11

Journey Five
2012

Journey Six
2013

Travel Photographer of the Year Collection

Many of the award-winning images from Travel Photographer of the Year are also available as postcards, greeting cards and exhibition quality prints, in the Travel Photographer of the Year Collection. The photographers receive royalties from the sale of these items, which are available from the online shop at **www.tpoty.com**

Visit **www.tpoty.com** to buy Journeys One to Six, or enter Travel Photographer of the Year for a chance to see your photography published in a future Journey portfolio.

Ninh Thuan Phan Rang Vietnam. **Nguyen Vu Phuoc, Vietnam.** *Nikon D3s with 70-200mm lens; f16; 1/1200s, ISO 800*